OTHER BOOKS BY PATRICK PRITCHETT

Burn
Antiphonal
Salt, My Love
Lives of the Poets
Reside

Gnostic Frequencies
Patrick Pritchett

SPUYTEN DUYVIL
New York City

My sincere gratitude goes out to the editors of the following journals, where earlier versions of some of these poems were first published: *Hambone, Colorado Review, LVNG, The Cultural Society, Bombay Gin, Square One, English Language Notes, The Modern Review, Morkville*, and *Ur-Vox*.

"The Reliques" and "Lyrics for the Book of Ariel" appeared in the chapbook *Lives of the Poets* (Potato Clock Press).

Special thanks to Forrest Gander, Fanny Howe, and Ingrid Nelson for sage counsel and encouragement.

copyright 2012 Patrick Pritchett
ISBN 978-1-933132-98-3
Cover art by Elisabeth Nicula, "Sense/Absence"

Library of Congress Cataloging-in-Publication Data

Pritchett, Patrick.
Gnostic frequencies / Patrick Pritchett.
p. cm.
Poems.
ISBN 978-1-933132-98-3
I. Title.
PS3616.R583G55 2012
811'.6--dc22
2011046052

Gnostic Frequencies

for Joe Donahue, Andrew Joron, Peter O'Leary, Lissa Wolsak

"Naming, in the realm of language, has as its sole purpose and its incomparably high meaning that it is the innermost nature of language itself. Naming is that by which nothing beyond it is communicated, and in which language itself communicates itself absolutely."

    Walter Benjamin

"The science of the music of words and the knowledge of their magical powers has fallen away since men invoked Mithra by a sequence of pure vowel sounds."

    Ezra Pound

"I said, 'there is mystery in this place, I am instructed, I know the script, the shape of this bird is a letter.'"

    H.D.

"the tone-leading of the vowels"

    Robert Duncan

"Hurrah for Euphony!"

    Ronald Johnson

Doctrines of the Lyric Body

Doctrines of the Lyric Body	1
Ariel Composes an Etude for the Soul of a Dog	3
Ariel on the Hope of Song	5
Ariel on the Truth of Writing	7
Ariel in the Marketplace	8
First Letter to Iamblichus	9
On Enigma	11
Of The One	13
Ariel on the Canoptic Signature	15
The Spectral Logic of the Temporal Folds in on Itself	17
Ariel at the Palace of Forgetting	19
The Poem of Fire	21
Second Letter to Iamblichus	22
Ariel on the Opacity of the Crystal	24
Two Songs for the Future Poem	26
To Be Two	27
The Structures That are Loss	30
Alastos	32
The Rescue Dream of Ariel	33

The Master of the Book

Of the Angel Who is Abyss	37
The Book of Drowning	38
Annals of the Tree of the House of Dust	39
The Lost Book	41
The Book to Come	42
Smoke's Book	43
The Master of the Book or, Excession	45
The Book of Radiant Sending	48

Exact Presence	51
Archive	53
Etude for the Monstrance of Nothing	54
Summer in the Street of Cisterns	55
The Books of Remembering	57
Lyrics for the Lost Book of Ariel	60
Shelley Unbound	66
The Earthly Afterlife as a Psalm by Hopkins	68
The Dream of Yeats	71
H.D. in Egypt	73
At the Chapel of the Grail Mass	75
Northumbrian Etude	79
Antiphonal for Frank Samperi	82
Underworld	90
To Master Duncan	92
Ark Dive	94
Nothing Repairs	96
Homage to the Skald	97
The Heavenly Tree	99
The Library is Burning (Letter to M)	101
Theurgical Etude for Nate Mackey	103

GNOSTIC FREQUENCIES

Thought's Smoke	107
Smoke's Thought	109
The Ghost of Words	111
Spoken to the God	113
The Reliques	114
On The Sensation of Tone	116
And now the calm sea rises—	117
Gnostic Frequencies	118
Gesture Towards a Glyph of Stars	120

A Song of Degrees (i)	121
(charity as enigma)	122
Pleasures of the Lyric Body	123
Tremble	125
A Song of Degrees (ii)	126
In a Somer Seson	128
A Song of Degrees (iii)	129
Envoi	131

Doctrines of the Lyric Body

Doctrines of the Lyric Body

First of all, it is whisper, rather than
light. A torched sibilance in the ear
a refrain not a shine, the earth
heathen with the tombs of
sacre coeur, their dismal fonts
their baptismal flights.

Absent music, language is
catastrophe.
Mere prose is grief before
the torn rose, the grain
of wood insane inside
the book's crooked pages.

Whatever is read there
is abandoned to trance
to the flowering silence
that folds the sign
engathering the sink
& pith of matter.
Resonant crystal directing
signals over impossible
distance. The *Cloud*
of song/the light tree
nested in stanzas of *shantih*
or whiteness, or candor.

Let the sinking of form
also be form — the mystery of
insatiate skin glowing with
the tendon of flame &
the story of its leaping over.
The shape of two crows, cruciform, in

the boat of their going over.
Beautiful, we say, a wing is destroyed
in its motion. But moving always.
As séance through scroll.
Bright amid the flare
of the letter, its folding.
Garment me, love, with the mere scrap of. Shadow.

Ariel Composes an Etude for the Soul of a Dog

In the Catalog of Minor Investigations, date uncertain,
    we find Ariel's assertion that
        the singular verb for being
            cannot be spoken.
    It haunts us
as the lights inside wine, or Orion's belt
    sheltered by clouds.

She goes on to observe
that of all our marks
    charis ξ
is the most cherished
because it enables
the world to continue.

The angelic, she avers, is a hollow
carved inside a kernel of wheat.
It disseminates a message about
the source of light.
(white light folded, sheathed
    about her, folded)

The Law of Emanation
proceeds & returns
    by the Force of Song.

Even the soul of a dog
                she remarks
abandons itself to gladness.

The reward of flame, plunging from the Pharos
                              is to flash out and disappear
        over endless water.

Ariel on the Hope of Song

     For the skull
is like a diamond, pierced
        with light and withholding it.
            Of its many griefs
Ariel says we must insist on a mode more extravagant
        than song
            but still issued in a form
     by which the notes will hold
        the tone.

Not mourning, she writes.
     (The entry is from the Fourth Ennead).
        Elegy, she seems to feel
     is too blunt an instrument.
            Because the radiance of the dead
is transferred by fire
     and there we may read (or so she suggests)
        the aurugenic properties of a midnight
            luminous without religion.

Then too
the doctrine of the subtle body maintains
     that passion is best treated as a propagation
  of waves.
        Ekstasis sounding
        through specific harmonies
           whose resonance

at twilight
signifies the dyad's perforation
and the gift of oil to the tree.
Made from tears, ascendant, primary, its colors bathe the collision
of the word & its sidereal double.
(Mead notes this too).

The chapter gives no indication
as to a progression of the Rays
or the *kathedra's* final disposition
after the brightness has abated.

A footnote, possibly in her hand
mentions a practice among certain Alexandrians
of building altars from the bones
of the ibis.
But it does not say what they who built them hoped to shelter.

Ariel on the Truth of Writing

The truth of writing
is in its disappearance.
That words are water
dripping syllables
from the oars till
the oars dissolve spilling
brightness from the instant in its fold.
Just as midnight reveals
the moon is only made of dust
so language mends the world
then wounds the mended.

I arrive at evening, singed by wind.
Set the table with fresh bread
look out the window
write a letter to my lover
send a wren to my lover
a bird sipping water.
I am tired of the book.
Tired of the lamp
and the rescue of oblivion.

Logos, we have said, causes
earth to rotate.
But distance strands every
prayer on the lip of astonishment.

Ariel in the Marketplace

She is identified in the surviving texts
primarily through the recurrence of certain tropes:

> "wing"
> "library"
> "seed"

So a ghost weaving the prowl of her own voice
> through the whirlwind of the
> *corpus symbolicum.*

"Devotion" she says, is a [   ] (possibly two words)
> & the light rescinds, [~~unbounded~~].

> > She strolls across the
> morning of the great festival, the sea close beside her
& the Grand Corniche strewn with petals.

All day long she opens the single letter ——
> the book that wrote itself
> > out of air, out of dust, from the heavy silt
> of beach fires and washed up wood
> > where the noise you hear is only
> the names and counter-names
> > a confusion of precision rhymed with the dead.

The Book, O Prince, is a dream of one white letter.

First Letter to Iamblichus

Iamblichus, my darling, the insensate world throngs us
        we are grief in its floodrush to ruin.
            Who will take passage through
                the doctrines of the Book
    gathering
the perfectible errors of our operations
                miming disfigurement
    to assail resurrection?

              (And who will come after us to burn
the ladder whose structure is motion, a dialogue of the one
    & the none?)

Sovereign as lake water
    reed-tasseled, serene
the Countenance haunts my speech
        with the mirror of the true dying.
Not this demarcation, but its bitter writing
        through
    to unravel night by a theory
        of horror
& mend the negative with the other
        of history.

            (No pardon till first we walk the Tablets
    by a sequence of pure sound).

But I am owned of love and its law is a star
        a flame for ascending the spine of the lighthouse
                announcing the knot of each
                        syllable.

        Alexandria, if you would mend the ghost
            be the author of a world.

On Enigma

In forgetting I join the lost
vigil
        keeping watch for the caesura
              that when it comes will cut us
        with the unhoped-for.

As a light that extinguishes all
        other lights
              yet retains their residue.

On the streets around the dock
the cry of "cool, cool" goes up.
Merchants selling oranges in the heat of day.
Their echoes fade in the empty square.

In the pages of the Book
        the lost things
        are kept *as* lost.
Kindling for *parousia*
        inside another word.

        The enigma of memory is that it exceeds living.
More than I see I misremember.
                Swim minnows
                      through shadowed pool.
                      Swans
                drift on the river.

You would hold me, too.
    There would be
                no
        other answer.

Of The One

How do we speak of one
              author when the multiple
instigates jokey parables
      of another
            mocking the edges
            of this one
                  as the moon clowns a pool
with images of itself?

Or what about
the wreckage of pathos as
                it woos us
           into wooing
and masks the entry
      to
the difficult, the tattered, innumerable
        psalms for disappearance?

"This is the place where the ghosts of Set and the monster he fights rage through the marble memory that is wrecked and rebuilt Marachek, the oldest city, forever."

We might say that The Book leaks the future.
That it compounds the odds for desire returning.
That it makes sport with the flags of other bodies
and that The One (if there is one) is only the other who swims
through wealth like someone strumming ruin.

Or
we might say that I am writing writing
and this is my Book and you are writing, too.
      (A small light goes on).

Why does the poem end, he asks.
Why is the poem always about loss?
About endings, about the impossibility
of ever having endings?

      For these meanings we suggest
      you consult some other work.
      This Book is not the one.

Ariel on Canopus & The Signature

You will walk by the great river
    but it will not be a river.
You will say "now it is midnight"
    but it is only the star overhead.

Soma pneumatikon and then what?
(Lapse of doves, paleologos fade out —)

    The world lightless speechless sealess
        worldless.

I cannot remember now what they looked like.

    Only this is real, my Master.
        Your strange technology
            for bringing back the dead
                inside of a book.

You have to hear (what).
    [The gnostic iron of the angel in her dress of sidereal cold]
    You have to *hear*
        whatever She will, even dead, mark upon the tablet.
        (Sigil, rudder, tear)

(the One has grown lost in the soul of an animal)

& then her Messenger, Who came to us day after day with her Signature
    (it lays glittering —)

She said (the candle poised above the pool in shadows):

Form poses the dead, is door & echo   through echo
    (*a* minus All Ways).

        Form, ignited
engulfs the body.
    First by song.
        Then by Tremendum.

Poem for the Dismembering of the Poem

This is the gorgeous, the lame, the ruinous
    planet of paradise falling
through rhyme as
    the speed of your voice
rushs the dysmorphic world
    oiled apparatus grounding
        sugar
    into dust.

It was never the true promise anyway, its winch
    of blue fire aglow above
        evening's breakwater.
    Rather the run of litter
out of which the free graves
    of sparrows are built.
From the dirt they still murmur their endearments.

Naïve messages about
        invasions from the future
bombard the region of the brain
    that governs pleasure.
            At zero hour commence
    the deletion of passwords.
The firewall shattered by
    the malware of lyric

until the poem, too, is wholly dismembered.

The Spectral Logic of the Temporal Folds in on Itself

                she writes, so that
grammar becomes a parable about decay
        & how each book makes a shadow to
trail after it.

        The Unwritten
                can only speak of hope
which is a wound we carry and learn to believe in.

        But if I enter the broken world
tracing the visionary company of
departed love & trailing what starves
then only by its logic
        can I link
each ghost to its aura of dust.

Which is also a letter:
nocturnal hosannah, inhuman vesper.

To be concerned with grammar
is to take up utopia.

To take up utopia
is to consider the mechanism
        by which it will
                one day
                burn us
                to the ground.

Ariel at the Palace of Forgetting

Here are the ashes.
The day is beautiful.
Recollection is what is meant by loss.

Or why not pour water endlessly through a sieve.
Raptus soliloquy
melt in astonishment

shiver through the book's
violet stanzas
late insatiable afternoon.

You revise the words, their drift enriches.
Their drift is what we have
when we have forgotten home.

The days are beautiful
and the graveyard of beatitudes
engraves the grain of history.

The thirst of the poor's
the impossible strain
the poet's song won't slake.

It is heartbreak to listen
and heartbreak not
to listen.

Israfel's horn
that's poised to sound
and does not sound

& will never sound
unless we make
some other kind of listening.

The Poem of Fire

But this is the poem, alive and burning.
The poem of fire, in the quires of its turning.

This is the fire, this is its home
alive inside its burning of time

and this is the time of the poem's burning
alive yet dying in the smoke of its quotes.

This is the smoke that could be home
the whirling, the failing, this is the hope

and the hope of the smoke is for a fire
composed of nothing but quotes.

This is the quote, ignited by smoke.
The smoke of the poem that fuels the fire.

The word as it turns, chanting the end
and this is that spiral, the poem that is failing.

The smoke of a choir as it slowly wavers.
The hope of smoke inside a quote of fire.

Second Letter to Iamblichus

Then what do we say of "spirit"? That it runs through
the body, ragged as a lamb? Or that it *is* the body,
the whole, the damaged, lashed limb to limbic,
    stem to star?
                    Its least, last meter breathing
dizziness right over the edge
    of the said —

                    But sadder than that, too:
a doctrine of bells spelling out mute tropes for exile.
    A calligraphy of dusk unwinding in a swirl
        of hope.

                          Amulet
against the cough of rough syllabics, the burial breath seeks
rises to fire, speaks the peak of a voice sung through
    a glass chamber.

    But is it *spirit*?
I cannot
    trace any of this, you understand.

What does spirit do for the cleft of the rose
when its spray of idolatry signals the end & the perfection
    of the beauty of this world?

                All those who, lonely in their colloquy
(sand, stars) consent to be the chosen, that other
       word for lost —

                And we say *this* is spirit, the singular
                      (the dead and the world they
                              float in)

                In the listing of titles you will find a chart
for labial elements: meaning the god who is at the tip of
       the tongue, who is (vanished) and still
       to come.

Ariel on the Opacity of the Crystal

    The crystal, almost invisible
    vibrates at the edge of light.
A filament that dreams of entering the archive
       & vanishing inside the Absolute
           or its *shadow*.

What's written is only
read inside flame
    or else ink thrown under the hull.
        Bitter, yet bright for the Thousands who work
      the work of immersing. Ah love,
        you must see that!

How we press down, scratch the Body of Aleph
      gouged force field
         whatever I bring you is not
        destroyed
but beyond grief or pain
    to come to the Unending of
the Orchard's weeping, where vowels shape the stars.
    Gash this road.
        It is paradise, nor are we ever
    out of it —

But the Book is built from the logics of loss.
    The law of form, not form itself.
          Milkweed the sustenance

a murmur of *melos*, theography against the world's darkening.
    One grain, slowly wet by water.
        An acorn of light.

There is no other plea than this – to amend the atoms
    the tears, the friends
        who are the Lyric Body and keep it
burning for the lamp
    & the King who sits alone inside
        the white apple of his room.

Two Songs for The Future Poem

      1.

Alive, as Ariel, I slept inside the book
And when I woke it was the day of the book
And the world inside of it, all interior
Seeing, gold-shined by the light of that name
And its signature, an earth with dark feet
And a river for speech, its writing of the script
We would teach and know one another by.
There is no life except in the word of it.
You are that dark Ariel of the name.

      2.

X is the poem that cries itself in syllables
And rises, spontaneous, artificial, a wave of
Sound since sound is the primary, the uttered
And most urgent theory of life.

The signifier-god, if he comes, says the nothingness
That always lies under us becomes us as music
As the ghosts of all those who made us and in music keep
calling her whispered alien cantos.

To Be Two
for Ingrid Nelson

Or the fire of love is a letter from the king
        a seizure in the shape
        of a rose.
Where the will to possess must also
        erase you.
I am gone from this planet.
        Uplink datastream
        now.

Or the fire of love is the uncommon name
        La bella donna
        Che cotanto amavi.
Drawing distinct pressures along a line
        of invisible pleasure.
The force to wound to harrow to kiss.
        "The stones themselves are
        burning."

Or the fire of love remains exterior
        to language
        a Rose
In the garden of the Rose
        gate of loaves & never.
No speaking of desire is valid without
        asking "How may I
        touch you?"

Or the fire of love will *streyne him by the herte* —
> *al sodenly a-swowne*
> in the whirligig of dream.
Server crash <unknown error>.
> Re-boot erotic software
to find that a fool
> & his transcendence
> are soon parted.

Or the fire of love alarms the world
> and its tongue into a great
> doxology.
That madrigal is most apt that will
> lift a white wing.
From skin to skin Wide Area Network
> all a-swarm in ethercloud
> array my touch & gaze.

Or the fire of love goes haywire
> a wayward nightingale
> devising the dervish
of syncope. In the hall of the archive the light of it
> lowers lips to a moan
and then. What measure will consecrate
> me as I am
> *gaudium* resurrection?

Or say that the fire of love is
> what cannot be
> contained.
"Those branches which were a-flame
> became red-rose trees."
If loosed then a wing
> that cries
> > inside a river.

How else will love astonish the hinge & poverty of living?

The Structures That Are Loss

The body
       of the letter, Ariel writes
       lives in the threat of its breath.
A text that never forgets
that what builds memory, also destroys it.

       Distilled into the seams
       of the letter a séance
              whorled,
       imprinted, dissolved,
       bereft —
       then doubled.

So you mark the place of the poem
dust unfurled across the tablet.
A knife dipped
in the ink of a glyph.

(The soul is rhetoric, she says.
A way to determine a theology of the particle).

So the structures of belonging are the structures of loss.

No origin.
Only the restlessness of the text.

Poured out like
water — if you
like.

Water in a temple erected to deserts.

Alastos

To forget you is to touch you all over again, setting hand
to wood, to whatever held trace of you, as the memory
of you is the approach of something
still to come
              what shivers in the mystery of its silk
and is poured out and never seen again except
by those who tender the fares for the Dead
and scepter the sepulchers with
a whiteness past whiteness

That is the light where, says Plotinus,
I lose myself
and all that I

remembered

The Rescue Dream of Ariel

Or
there is a deeper chord
running
in hints through

    the mornings
    & evenings
    of the world

Vast
as a leaf
is vast

    & silver
    or maybe blue

Underground
of my love
    superb
    in the chant
    of its rhythm

So standing to sea
from the single perch
looking out

    Light ablutes

deranging
the stone with a flower.

The Master of the Book

Of The Angel Who Is Abyss

Go, sundering Book, echo of a vast disturbance.
Inside the smallest of your letters spill then spell
the secrets of how the Resurrection Gate builds the lyric body.
The heaviness of sleep thrums inside a fountain of nerves
and only the book about the Book may awake
or sever us as run to the doom of its embrace.
Form fades into paper and the shining bird who sang it
sings from the shade for the disappearance of the poet.
Then The Angel Who Is Abyss, who says the Book
must contain all existence, prises the beating heart
from the cradle of its slurried chamber
announcing *I am the hour make me pure.*
In the ceremony of evening nothing is complete
until the poem, too, is wholly dismembered.

The Book of Drowning

Is the book where reading is séance.
>   The eye flickers over
>   flickering letters
>   white in their paper evening.

>   (A single letter saturates the eye)

If the soul is harmony, as Plato says,
then the scroll will be what
>   disturbs. Emerging from the archive
the way fire grows from
>   wood.

I am concerned with facts which may belong, says Ariel Breton,
to the order of the pure, but which present all the appearances
of a signal, without being able to say
which signal —

It is, therefore, not
the end of dreaming
>   but another chapter
in the catalog of the *pharmakon*
>   the one liquid with the promise
>   of lyric.

>   Other word for disaster.

Annals of the Tree of the House of Dust

To read the Book backwards
go blind along an hour
of descending blossoms
hold incendiary twilight
       (crown of desire)
hold
the monstrous hero who
performs epic infusion
sails to another shore
breaking the bright ring
of *nostos*
           for the sweat
of the beautiful instant
of loss & circumference.

Said Ariel:
    "The sun who dwells and guts
    whose answer is an altar designed for emptiness
    — the sea of a million *nella miseria*
           carry
    the documents of my gaze
    past bones & prayers

           Speak
    as I land at the kingdom
    of the irreducible
    gold filtered between green boughs.

>   For landing
>   is falling
>   & falling
>   a going beyond."

As the pawn sparrow
on a destitute branch is
the godly lodestar of spring
in its loneliness
>   so the neural net-weave
>   refolds
catastrophe inside
the ten nodes of the tree.

>   *Who enters speech abolishes distance —*
>   *Brings us near, as near as breath —*

Keter to *Tiferet*
the green grass
bends in the house of dreaming
elder sign of desired shore
oars dipped in white fuel
blades for the keening.

The Lost Book

Only fragments of the Book That Was Lost remain — yet what is loss
except another way to keep the whole while giving it away?

Logos (she hints) runs wild, continually unraveling the One. Think of becoming
as a kind of ruin, she urges, soaking the poem with strange nutriments.

Neither drone nor seizure but a melody of the serious green
things and the world they embrace in the act of seeing.

Entranced, as an opening made by dream, the last few flakes
of flame fall through the edges of whatever we were saying.

Whatever we were saying glows transparent
till it's lost in evening's layers of haze.

As the names announcing matins only increase the void.
Aspirant with longing, they shine because they are empty.

The Book to Come
for Anna Deeny

   In the book of the
world to come, when what we wish for
    is only to build things
   by singing —

            In that book,
where the watery pages save the weed of a word with a wing
the future wavers, its theater of the visible like a map
lit by a match
      and the summer night spherical with
      the hope that signs every trope
          to its meaning
          in the world.
Offered up, this once, simple as
        a feather.

   The words falling and unfolding
over the words we have been waiting to say.

Smoke's Book

The smoke of the book after great labor
gives off a scent of evening.

It is sweet to read there among a confusion of letters
where a sparrow is also an Angel
  come down chanting
  psalms for the unbearable
  bell of a tulip
  pitched one degree
  beyond silence.

Say I read through the night and into whiteness
& say I am both ointment
  & a reef on fire
  a ship off the coast
& a scribe of the text's darkness
baring my arm, my face
  my entire work
  to the unbearable sun.

Whoever would quench me
drowns in a glade of light &
whoever then reads me
  bears limit
  like a cup
  for endless refilling.

Who writes me, rewrites me.
    Makes a history of
    care, marking all
    my errors as eros.

The Master of the Book or, Excession

A god spoke to a king, he said:

> *Radiant excession dawns.*
> *To cast asunder*
> *is to affirm its vowels.*

"And rhetoric?" asked the king.

Never better.
Then he smiled.

*

"Are the dead all neophytes?" asked the king.

{a g o d h e s p o k e a l l i n a m b e r s i g n a l s h e r e}

> *You mean are "the dead" as you so ghoulishly call them*
> *still as stupid as they were in life?*

"Well, yes."

> *Let me tell you a story.*
> *Once there was a man named Bertolt Brecht.*
> *No, that won't do.*

"?"

To inquire of me means launching phantom datastreams
means further dissonance
irradiates
all Sectors.

Dot *
Dot *
Dot *

The dead
are the real and the dilation
of the real.

Bell & signature, quick dissolve
the key
to Sublimity only this:
"I am meaningless, lying here, foundational, a kernel."

Null dataset. Cosmic foam.

Loss not the source of meaning
but the threat
of disappearance
makes the Song
rise.

*

And he added: {Light steeps the body in the visible effects
of gravity, which as Newton knew, is the
demonstration of God's *caritas* in the world}.

*

And:

Let khora *stand for*
      [   ]
        the wave that is running

                      and let the wave
at the edge of the random train its halo over
                                excession

Let Excession be the myriad junction
                      of implicate folds
             so tendered

*

Post-script:

> "For so the Eternal Delight comes to be perceivable, and this perceiving of the unity is called Love, and is a Burning or Life in the unity of God; and according to this Burning of Love, God calls himself a merciful loving God; for the unity of God loves and pierces through the painful will of the Fire, which at the beginning rose in the breathing of the word, or outgoing of the Divine Delight, and changes it into Great Joy."
>   Signed, Jacob Boehme

The Book of Radiant Sending

"My dear Thoth-Hermes,
    You tell me of
various galactic intrigues:
        the fall of Sargon
        the despair at Antares
        the latest fashions among the Rigellians.
But what of the Hallows
    & its residual cluster
    of unsubdued light
that radiates still?
    What
    of the Subtle
    Body?

The fuel of the fire, O my King
is the world on its altar
turning.
Excendence – to rise out of –
is a falling further into
the subtle body, itself a kind
of A R C H I V E
held
as a form of always running,
the combustible quanta
of the poem
as it seizes
flares all around you.
Prayers, ghosts

chaunts
apocalypse
& the spinning wheel
in the organ formerly known
as the heart.

"Thoth, that these things are or were or continue
       somehow —
 that they collude
at a point beyond
     the visible horizon —
that even as we speak here at
      End-World-Time
All this, I say, is not
   The Sign
  but an instance of that deeper
burning whose moment allots us
  our silver & all our
  yearnings for excendence
    transparent."

Each phenomenon
given as it
is –
riven
shattered,
discomplete –
make no motion at all
without reference
to the frame of

a Larger Becoming
by which completeness itself
is always the articulation
of a radical locality
that is, incomplete:
a pocketful of poseys.

"And then?"

The thirst
of the Subtle Body
saturates
a natal register
of tears.
Connection
is labyrinth.
Event horizon
shimmer.
Then, rain.

"Byss. Wisdom. Tincture.
The Three Exalted Properties.
Kingdom of Love, Light, Glory.
    Which only now can be
    understood as an Object
    a Radiant Sending."

<----[end transmission]---->

Exact Presence

"Exact presence whom no flame can ever again hold back"
      I turn in you as Thoth turns
communicating what I cannot as yet see
its governing wavelengths broadcast
      on the narrowest of bands
      its archangelic photons emanating
the discharge of *hyperousia* which is itself a black body
      form of radiation hovering
much as a ship hovers suspended above a crystal of pure water.

About you there is nothing at all exact because form
      grows forever multiple shadows
out of its shifting presence. They bewilder us, we are
aghast, shivering in the daydream between arches
      where the cold run of excession
      trembles in the zero
of its own regard — striking signals, silence
      the greater ward of that mission
to ignite the parables of a green earth inside *mysterium tremendum*.

Datacluster, netweave, neural fire bearer.
      Crow as dawn sips migrant
      toxins for the sundering
of a fever & the body of delirium, its wreckage
named I-burn-over-midnight & marked by whose hands?
      Instant of the supply
      harrowing my sister
her wild stare to afternoon another river or.
Is it the strange among us, inside us, chanting misery/pulchritude

Hosannah flare-dust in the afterglow?
        Ship of all degrees
point of wheeling light & a seizure of the left hand
in its sensorium canopy, come as far as the sound
        of bees over a field
        of grass & snow.
Revolve in your finitude as the form of longing
        over many years
traversing arc of skull, vibratory prayer & threshold.

Archive

And then the small books
without witness.
Ghosts
patching history.

Wanting clairvoyance.
The othering toward
a new moored
shore.

Wanting lumens
at springtide
& the city singing
in green wheat.

Unspanned
surge of green
vowels.
Utopian chasm found.

Etude for the Monstrance of Nothing

And I reach the Book
        and it is broken into blossom.

        At the place
        where loss & structure
        become
        the same thing.

        As a little bridge of grass
        is a late beginning
        to the stars.
        Uttering the monstrance of summer.

But then to go beyond
        the white book
                seeing to the edge
                of the alphabet
        that is endless.

The long plunge
        to form is continual.
It is nothing, I say, nothing
                to fall into the Book
        or to pray without ceasing for the company of unknown
names.

Summer in the Street of Cisterns

Because the vessels will never be able to contain
        the Abundance

the cascade of
        radiance that
        pours out from
        the breaking
        of the Book
to cover the length of the street and overflow its dust
        with dust.

Enter random search query:
            Semiotic whispers as
            the algorithm for repletion.

    &
the dawn gone to swanned rust —
    &
the Sum of Hosannahs draining away —
    &
the nakedness of speech
shedding its words
        one by one.

By ruin I climb ruin.
The Book's catalog of sorrows
its emendations, its erasures.

Gazing out on what, after us, is
      a scripting of
          impossible flowers —

The Books of Remembering

      1.

In the spring, the city is full of gods.
They speak in the sun and the scent of absinthe leaves.

In the silver of the sea, the blue room of sky
in the whiteness of the streets, the trees alive with birds.

Here entire faiths arise out of words
for a king's disappearance.

Nocturnes for the gaze which singed us.
The rain-touch of fever that turns our friends to stars.

But to cross out the world
with the promise of a World?

It must come back to Song — lumens, love & the names
for the double-flicker of what resists & resurges.

"Maintaining the enigma
in the void of its answer"

means irradiating each splinter
in its stanza of wood.

My love, an archive is only
the d/ark in the moment of any speech.

2.

And how did they
burn the books?
They burned them
in each of their letters.

And how did they burn
the vowels and their worlds?
They burned them from *domus*
to *cantus*, from smoke to rune.

Did they burn the stations
of their discontaining?
In the house of smoke the ghost
of the book rises above the last ember.

A ghost is only a voice
exhuming disruption of desire
giving to negation
the persistence of hope.

Where the book turns wood
into flame and flame into emerald
there a wing gives I to *I* .
And there all the planets drop in the Sun.

Day unto day uttereth speech.
Where the twenty-six fragments
are burning in the brightness of foaling
each into each.

Lyrics for the Lost Book of Ariel
for Tim Morton

"Corporeality is the goal of the ways of God" — Friedrich Schelling

1.

It was Ariel who walked the blue shards
And spelled the ligature of the fall and its foaling.
Ariel who beheld the ruin of the body
In the body's morph and prism.

The gulf of days was a bell and its echo
Calling across the bones of the sea.
Ariel sang beyond every genius
And she was burning as she came.

Like a glass poured into a river
She unbequeathed all signatures.
The star that hung its light for her eyes
Crowned her hair with the sign for abandon.

O come by wand, by cup, by nothing.
Like a halo, like a flicker, like a bomb.
Who will release the melligenous song
Of the last of the day that discompletes us?

Or say the instant of this shattering
Deletes the running of form and becoming.
Say she is nowhere but the frame of dissolving
And we are the wreckage of her bourne and her wake.

2.

Ariel says:
the dance is
of a world gone
to the edge of its
own light.

She says:
the ode and what
breaks it
measure the same
thing.

3.

Ariel broke the book in two.
The sentence inside spoke,
        it said:

Language comes as a sign beyond all others.
The of-itself reaching out to another.

Like love, its energy pervades
all that it touches.

It cannot hold enough.
It is here and over. Endless.

4.

Lyric, says Ariel, is the barcode of the dead.
It mourns us into dreaming.

But to be given over to the other
is as smoke from an arrow

or music out of a goblet of apples
when all the guests have gone home.

5.

Ariel murmurs *thalassa*
not as Xenophon did
but for the dove whose light singes
all who see it.

The dove is requisite
a burning into time.
Its wings are shadows
inside a white fire.

The mother of the dove
is the earth in its turning
saying we cannot
not praise our own becoming.

The hard thing is to be awake
under stars nor to drown
their sparks in a flood of words —
dream-specter in the chorus of hooded glory.

The issue of tears is the great form of desire.

6.

Ariel drinks and says:
*The night in which all cows are black
is only the sweetness of a form unseen.*

She does not enter as the answer
to your poem.

Wine and the darkness of day descend.

7.

Grass is a crown, she says, it goes beyond bitterness.
It makes the bones of the sea satellite, radiant.

Ariel burns in her dress and she burns supine
and she says (she says) *I will be your idol.*

8.

Ariel says:
the Pure Land is a fragrance
& a breath I learn to say
& unsay.

The stain of the body
grows its crystal — involution
mounting to a height
unguessed.

A clod of clay
that deepens each day.

It spreads out across the four worlds.

9.

To shed the doctrine of the Blind
you must first go by way of the unseeing.
Holy is the night in which all cows are black,
by which occlusion narrows the focus to a single bead.

The vision of a dawn hangs by a thread.
To see me by the grain I am & uttered whole
enter through the sound of bells.
The brightness of the scission enfloods the eye.

Or else the hood of glory is a singing also
in the narrowness of the body's prism.
Become what bleeds away, what casts
its flare to the shore of thigh & finger.

The ultimate of Wheels rolls in gold and stutters
as the farness of the sundered comes
to hold us in a tide of revolving lights.
Gaudy Ariel, the rapture encants us one cell a time.

Shelley Unbound
for Jeffrey Robinson

We have journeyed toward the beyond
                which is an atmosphere all its own.
                    Made of vibrations or particles
    and the forgiveness of that debt
                that is a kind of ruined arch
                besides which sits a blonde woman.
      She knows our names
             & all our abysses
    and who lives in our houses
    and she says that the things we give off
         must be electric.

                 Everything that shines
with its own light
         subjoins us to some hour when
            the city goes all blue
            and
what I know of the sea is not scraps and patches
      but this endless talking
           in which I shall meet you
like a wild swan
       shivering in the wideness of
            exertion.

But the vanished world looks back at us
              and we grow smaller.

There is a castle and then
                              a gulf
and we know we cannot yet come home.
          To think of the boundary without thinking
                  of touch?
     When your write you send account
          of rains and the number of crowns
                and the boat of the actual
                      that is passing continually.
     For a word is a species of enclosure. The iron bar
and residence of a thousand forms all arriving
            on the same day.
  Justice is nothing unless it is first
                a beautiful translation.

The Earthly Afterlife as a Psalm by Hopkins

What is water
        but the body's sigh
                lapping around the body?
In its green diocese
        I swam until
                I went under.

By wave, by wood, by bone
        you accrued the sayings
                for the afterlife.
Till their measure
        poured out morning —
                threshed grain of birdsong.

        Under-sky
                by flank of grass
my lord's sweet palace shivers.
        Disheveled
                beside the ruin
of a sundown hour.

If I could match by script
        the grammar
        of the strummed heart's fables of disaster
then I might blend
        the ruth of living
        with the iron furnace

        of vespers.

        Alive on earth
to the least contour
        we shape every ridge & hollow.
The green unfixable river
        that prays us
            as we surge headlong
            into calamity whirlwind.

Take these minutes
        from the log
of song's darkening toll.
    From the pulse
        & pause of a day
and its silted up
        wind-jacked sorrow.

Where the bitterness
        of the daily harrows each alone
        for the sake of love
that is ending
        and never gone.

Where the evening tree
        recalibrates the ache of a star
            in its lonesome pine pinnacle.

*Poem, my body, go amid the flotsam
as the diamond that is none or all
someone's daughter laughing
spilling brightness from her mirror
sundering the wideness of the field
from lamp to tree, cleft to chapel.*

The Dream of Yeats

And the women who burned
Shelley's body

did they burn the book of shadow
& all its letters?

Did they write their names
as music sliding out of sleep

& strewn with broken figures?
Were their heads circled with light?

Being dead, did they rise
as swans and so create

the final reach to
translunar paradise?

Because I speak death joins
joy to the intercourse of light.

The soul in the evening walks
beside my love. The soul is a song

that forms the body with a look.
Now an apple cups its poise of dew

and all the grass is gone to shivers.
Death, ruin Earth, then go past ruin.

But an apple for my true love, who walks
through evening, the green stain of its furnace.

The soul is what they say
cannot stop from singing.

Grass, what goes through Avalon
ravenous, its cold green water running.

H.D. in Egypt

So it was nothing, nothing at all
the first words that found me
perfecting the Mysteries

as a circlet may break
in the heat of the poem's fire
and a boat carry the beloved

to the place where we read by starlight.
My sign-posts are not yours
but may my words help you, traveler

as you cross this uncertain land.
The darkness is only archive,
the spirit of the Book that keeps us.

Alive in its promise we see the reach
of earth extending, the body of light
become the body of flesh

the signal speaking the whorls
of poesis, the madness of the world
falling down around our ears.

I do not remember the prayer or command.
I no longer can recall what the Message said.
All I know now is carried in song —

that we must burn as we live
ignited of Ship, and croon and sway,
and never forget.

At the Chapel of the Grail Mass
(David Jones)

    1.

"Who under the green tree
had awareness of his dismemberment."

Who even then held vigil
      as of a continual Mass
a theater of the messianic
      where the bright cup
fills the bones with fire
& the pressure of the name
      hallows each limb
      with a splinter —

Who tends to the hawk
must also heed the shadow of its wave,
that dreams the earth
until the Great Queen awakes
her Sophianic flare
      a whiteness beyond white
& the harbor naked in the moonlight
      churning what the heart
      cannot keep.

At the threshold
of form a sparrow

comes running all dirt
      and flutter.
Gone straight to croon —
      to chapel-garth &
unshuttering – white flame of
      Whitsunday fluttering.

By this sign will you cast
your letters into the fire
the mystery of matter
alive in an hour
that is always burning.

      Oblivion or
pearl?

      If you go to the Grail
then, go brag a thousand miles.
In deep rain enduring
the actual as it unfolds
a story about "an appearance
purely of itself."

Or else take the stoning road to an eastness
      past ending,
consenting to be the accomplice
who receives this message,
the witness inside a lavishing
of mortal soil that is this strophe.

      On that day
a lark rising and a sun straight
out of Albion
will ravage our blindness
till we see as the fleeing do:
    The terrible
inseparable from the chord
      of love inside it.

2.

At Whitsuntide
the ancient emeraldings.

The tongue impaled
on a spike of white fire.

And afterwards who walked there,
a little flame, like a caress?

Speak of the turning year & its descent
in which we enter utterly to turbulence

glad in the whirl of it
making a natal music.

A lamb who sang beyond sorrow
the little Songs of Degrees.

Who lauded and magnified
the stars in their frolics.

Who gave back from first grammar
benignity, singing

from the green shiver
in the throat.

Or by tears melted out of Albion
forged a first orthography.

Hammurabi, dial sundown.
Lear-sea, blow over.

Northumbrian Etude
(Basil Bunting)

You will plumb the line
        from fathom to Morpethshire.
            Eke out of gray slate
                ode's entablature.
    Bitter on about a quarrel and its two bright
        swords.
            Or how the meaning
    of a song
        is carried along
    in the swoop
        & fold of
        its music.

Take measure of
        the Pleistocene animal, strident of
        grass & snow,
    whose starburst vocables strafe
        the belltower's wet skull
            as it zones the town
                around
            administering precincts of
            sound.
    But underneath the Zodiacal clock
        each breathes the air
            he would call
            his own.

                    Field running
widdershins
        down to the last bone. Who, hefting
                stone, runs the green wear of
                        it past caring?
                                Or does Caedmon's
        licorice lyric translate
                        to rougher tones
                                the shimmer-stammer mandate
            of Enochian frequencies?

Strum and candle,
for a lord walks in shadow.
Strum and soft anchor,
a star at the edge of sight shivers.

Let the fools of the world spend at will
                crazed monuments
            for the batterings
                of time. The mitre cannot rule
the river, nor the belltower upend
                one syllable of song
                for the making of
                    the day,
                its flare-encradling
                        apple-drenched
                        drop.

The priests go rattling on nohow declaiming codes:
panics & alerts
    for draping the horizon,
        hanging the black canopy
    to save their investitures.
Still, the little stars shine
        through.

    Who was Tamburlaine? A great horn
        sprawled flat
  in the grass.
        Now song rises into the very arc
        & dent of a hammer.
          A blue spoke
            stood up plain
          against the sun.

Antiphonal for Frank Samperi

        1.

Now they wood the bright
they river the great house
launch the body of incontestable
                light.

        XPISTOS
        harbinger
        daily the
        wing-run.

To be on a bridge is to scatter love, love.

        Is to scatter
                the longing for failure
                        across the seven languages
                as the word for angel
                      is whirling.

Drowning
        or beyond-ascent.

2.

Come by wing, magnify such song
the way glass in autumn burns & trees
sweep through deep fire, sourced
in quickness of water.
Asunder among sparrows, dust
of the dried fuse exhaling
the winnowed grain
threshold of particles, seeding
streets and prayers and homes.
Thunder on the prairie for the door of spring.
Diamond groan antiphonal.

3.

By the waves
        anew tune.

Elemental
        the green hand

runs its veins
        through raged grove.

The outset
        commingles

light with nave
>	grass with a charm

so the dead
>	might burn & see.

Gaze over land
>	the stone flume

of moon, its
>	high-dial

spun to blue.
>	Dawn arch

poem-wracked.
>	Sophia

demonstrance.
>	Bright terrace

soon supply
>	lorded swoon.

    4.

The eyes grow bright with the room's dimension.
        The ontological is a
    proposition.

        What, it asks, does
the beautiful carry?

    5.

It is
not this day
its wind
hover
motion
its stillness
inside tree
vein
its
standing
wave
but more
uncertain
still

the knowledge
of nocturne
at noon
and at noon
the brightness
of the
walls
attesting
the lesions
of song.
Give as
equipped
for the sundry
dives
the raggedy
body
asleep in
sunlight
or the system
of the aesthetic
a sphere
of
poverty &
surprise
poverty for
the great coat
of heat
that melts
us in our pride.

6.

Last known configuration.
    Appled with mitre
  of birdsong.
    Windtrough
torque
  of breath
infusing
  candled contagion.

To remedy forsake the known.

Plunge migraine acre
  to loss.

    The soul
  is a speck
    of pollen.

7.

System restore?

  The grain of
  the real
  says

the new
by eluding
it.
Past
clarity
& more than
surplus
it subsumes
the ache
at the center
the soaked
kernel
by which
finitude
saddens
the sign
of Sunday.
Instance
upswing
waters.
The singular
kiss
darkens
the entire body.
It scrapes
signs to
the bone.
Heaps
form
on the

furnace.
Makes of
light ever
center
opening
out &
beyond.

Underworld

(i.m. Denise Levertov)

1.

Calm of midwinter's day.
How we live in it
the blinding glare of sun
on ice, its demands like
Vivaldi's "Gloria"
too rich and impossible
to meet all at once
but taken in by parts
by the median satisfactions
of "just living"
the way wood is worn in the groove
of its use
and the ancient nerves of the hand
respond with the inchoate tremble
of affection for all this
bitter largesse
its avidity under starkness
its mute enchantment with the Sayable
the smoke of it rising above
the stripped-out trees
the non-descript homes
here in the underworld.

2.

Enter low
as the weeds command it.
As the plain edge of sky everywhere
abrades it, the passage
between one world
and another
dormant
equivocal.

The monstrance of seeming
seeming to bear
nothing
but the grazed
bell of longing in
mid-air
its sleek syllables sending
the throat of this day
and the night to follow

                                      afloat
on the wavering paper
the consubstantial hegira
that is this forest
this river
and is running
as it is running

& is nowhere.

To Master Duncan

Ship leaving or arriving of my poem
you plunge past speech
        past touch
                past earth.
        To a room of water like sky
& the book of stars growing old.

No one can save brightness
        from its ruin
or the instant from its need
                for suddenness.

Telluric mediums rave
over ghostly liturgies
& I call on you to save yet
        you cannot
only the bitter lave of the poem
        to wash the green of
        your first reading.

The intelligence that sings
each tree to wakefulness
destroys both ground and root.

AS TO THE PLACE
        where the body is drawn out
& Abides love comes
              in a music of utter strangeness

        and the wrecks we found nearby glowed so that
        what was loss was also the drag of stars swept
        in the slower drag of prayer

From the startled instrument of its calyx
        a rose scans the weather for dust
        & the rose will be the agent
for the conjunction of *Solis et Lunae.*

As why I risk the other light — its aptitude for
        forgiveness. Its underside where
            our errors turn decay to
                retrieval.

Ark Dive
(i.m. Ronald Johnson)

In ark-dive,
grey encomium.
Grey imperium of
the all-day rust-dawn
-ed day.
If amen, then a willow
& its sibilance too.
Or water bluster
in stone-cracked creek.
Force of lone stone empty
on an earth swept
wide.
And stricken by
late winter-sun-and-lance.
By this tide, great gong:
ever-and-a-going,
gone.
We go so — in measure-
less tread, dividing
song from wing.
Particle-cleave, (parousia)
your run is ended.
A nascent valence
resumes.
Foremost among foot-
falls and sober

in Elysium to be going
if light there is ever sober
or windonsea any-
thing but claritas,
supra urbem, supra sapientia,
bells building spire
on spire in the true
font of soul's un-
encrypted in-
scription.

    (Hover a while.
    Breathe this and be glad
    of it.

NOTHING REPAIRS
(i.m. Robin Blaser)

  That each perceives the hidden in what form they can, in a form they make their own/ as when a star at certain intervals hurls its energies outward/ the void collapses then remits light as matter and light is what remains

  continuously it feeds/ sustained through waves of repletion and emptiness, but always a hunger, the weakness of god before what already is, an image of the undone whole wrapped in the spell of all it has devoured

  That each takes up ritual, its kindness, multiple voices emitting & perishing into echoes/ a kind of dance, intricate polyphony, as seeing is salt to song, the wound and what it decrees/ harbor and the little orisons floating for the millions lost to

  seed/ Abandoned, they drift over arctic air chanting pagan cures *you should take care not to die* or be as one who dreamt last night the stars fed our hopes/ they spiked our bones into jeweled cabinets

  That the cause of the light be the same as what it touches/ companion to the hand still writing from the dead & setting down again the last syllable that will not fall falls now/ the shining vowels spelling out what is the word for soul, I said "master"

         the light remains

Homage to the Skald
(for Ken Irby)

And for the dreaming, the endless
mode of occurring
as it is, as it could be, as the sleepers
keep murmuring —

    for what it means
    to stay alive, attuned, a moment
    to this *otherwise*
    & the sought-for, disappearing.

Of pure possibility/of the nothing
that may save it
shed of symbol, it staves off
the blighted, and so we go – into night

    the blessed, the earthly
    what leaks into & wrecks us
    is always
    never and more singular than loss

across song's fields, folded. Inside its portals
the old book beckons and we bend
surmised of sorrow, to its rising, it turning.
What dies &

what inherits? What dissipates
and what is remnant?
If the wind is not/if the wind is here and —
its inconstancy, its minglings, its slips of

>   substance into light and
>   into beginning
>   for beginning is always.
>   *Begin again.*

The Heavenly Tree
(for Gerrit Lansing)

Tree
waking in the
radium of twilight
the O of stone on its knees
    in water.

The dominion of God is a ~~shattering~~
        under rain
where grass is an easter of sparrows
        enflamed
            the *sacre coeur*
    of a mansion in
        the branch of pine.

If tree as darkness
then also the *raptus* of sun —

    Edge
where to dwell is to become so
        beautiful.

Golden with the daylight of fawn
& green lallation of earth's ink.

As
lovers
will dissolve
and coagulate
in a river
praising
all they hold to
& abandon
finitude brightened
by the sweetness and sooth
of affray.

And this is the chariot.

The car of light beneath the tree of stars.

The Library is Burning (Letter to M)

The Library is burning
>floor by floor

and in the flames
the books open
their pages

>uncontainable —

Plume and vortex

>Or else
the wounded are
elected to the crystal
distilled
>of a cinder —

>In my dream I see it
falling through itself
the books and the pages
falling through them
>and all the words
>falling out of the
>words

The greater masters of regret
bent over their instruments
      shearsmen of sorts

When, I asked, is the Library
not burning?

Theurgical Etude for Nate Mackey

The song, spun, and
at the end of it, un-
      done.
As the archive,
      its pages in ruin
rewrites the myth
of its own demise
      abides
in it, the flat
octaves mounting
      to the sky.

Undone,
as music
      bleeds in the wide
      eyes of the Bride.

      The steps she climbs
so so, so swift, as
      certain as tide
      & tide falls

with the rumor of
      a ruin of time –
so her steps, re-paced,
      measure the bright
      stairs, in

       stars of cadence,
              each
       a prayer, the whole
       song of it splayed
              & broken
           re-opened
       to the page of white
           letters,
       each letter
           begetting

       a further begetting
           & from the ruin –
       this song, done, at
           the end of it,
               not done.

Gnostic Frequencies

Thought's Smoke
for Teresa Villa-Ignacio

So I was thought, she
thinks (not thinking)

So I was spoke, she
says (not spoken)

and the day room
swept by a full

moon and the curtain
unharmed by a breeze

it is autumn
someone said —

under the leaves
and the moon lies under

autumn, she
murmured, who

will be the last
to sit down

to table & speak
as speech that is smoke

leaks out who will hold out
hope for the ghosts

that they sweeten the meal
or be the first

to come out and look
as the moon falls through the west

as it slides, as it goes
under the leaves?

Smoke's Thought

So the book was smoke
smoke's drift, a cloud

that was broken
on a sky so blue

so the wind spilled
the sun, the sun

running over stanzas
Blue will you

echo the kindness
of the reader

and her grain of sand?
Will you stain

the book and its
blackened moment

the page and its error
of swans

lapsed
along the margin?

To be smoke
is to go anonymous

sublime as the keel
of a boat-under-whisper.

By magnifying loss
we have made a map

of the stars.
But not the dust

that is smoke &
drifts in between.

The Ghost of Words

What is essential
is a Ghost made of words
set before the ghostliness
of living
that is also
our innermost
story about
the poverty
of forms
and what they give
she said.
To shine we must be
disordered
along a line of
other words
and to sing
means eking out
primitive sonorities
entreating the withheld
from the smallness
of its nouns.
What is
central to my love?
Assumption
of all loss as
caress.
Bestowal

over water
cradle of
accosting
every echo.
All the enigmatic
evenings of
the seared world
come running
to set their octaves
here.
Archiving ruin as splendor
(dazzle) (blind) (mote) (surrender).
This is the ruin of the mortal
calling you from
inside its fever.

Spoken to the God

If I fall asleep it is the city I sleep of
its arches, its ramparts
the blue desire of its spires.

And if the structures of
words overheard in sleep
fray in the vertigo of devotion

I will be inside them too
and inside the rooms of the words
that write their history there.

When you go to the gate
you will carry your clothes
and whatever you know

about the action of light on objects.
You will walk through the streets
and spend the cure of the ground

and sleep in the straw of silence.
You will live with the skill of the thief and feed
the dream of the word with words.

The Reliques

The Reliques of many lie like the ruins
of all parts of the earth. Last valediction over
bones. Beyond Theatrical vessels & voices silently
exceeding the dead the King figures some hope
of an Original, a compleat peece made up
of the Centos of all ages. Out of an extract of the earth
comes their owne depth and light. As water was
the orignall of all things so to conclude
is moist relentment.
       Others say
the proper Fuelle is winde, dust to be burnt
in their lives as books for the resurrection
even as the doctrine of Heraclitus composes
by finall pyre. But neither bones nor oil
neither Opale nor the Sepulchral Cells
of Pismires shall answer how the bulk
of a man should sink into volatile salt
or transmuteth as good burning light
in the Metropolis of humidity.

         Wherein
the bones of Musicall Instruments speak of simple
inhumation & therefore restless inquietude
stirs the diuturnity of our names into
the urging of carnall composition.
For the number of the dead so surpasses darknesse
as to be lost in the night of nothing

entering as the flame we live by
into the common particle.
       Invisible
it burns wood, pitch and mourner alike
in a rapture of liquefaction. Ready to be any
in the extasie of being ever, whereof all things
are but a colonie, obscure
in the Chaos of pre-ordination.
The taunt of Isaiah is an exolution
  & a glory.

On The Sensation of Tone

What is peculiar is undulant motion.
As when from a point in calm water a ring
advances outwards in all directions.

That the waves advance and do not return
but in their going compose a motion that disturbs
each particle it touches, propagating a sphere of tremors.

So when we strike the air with our voice
the words set off resonant shivers
vibrations passing as waves of sound to the ear.

To draw such curves for these sounding bodies
is to line the mouth of the poem with the Octaves
and the secrets of their dividing measure.

The speed of particles makes one single degree
of excitement out of the crest of the waves
of greater and lesser magnitudes.

And the sum of this action, rich with the voluble
shock of accord, lifts each stone and particle
through the shape of a wave we will call song.

And now the calm sea rises—

Speak spells into sparks.
Seamarks fade into phosphorous.
Seascape, needle's I

        The wound travels through the body of a man
        and the sea washes over
        the cargo of tawny gods
        their slang afoam with stories
of necklaces, jasmine, breasts and the heat of the dance.

        We are built out
        over the sea, they say.
        Our sails like iron
        under the imperious wind.

And the swimmers grasp the rungs of water dissolving in their hands.

Gnostic Frequencies

Imagine this, murmur as murmur only just
this much of white's whiteness
giving body color. Cold the blue eyes
now the white insists it grows older
together but never what it is imagine this.

Imagine this, murmur. Color and no body.
Color and no bird fixes the light of its song to a branch.
Color and not all white. As murmurs, as pulses.
Feeling the séance of matter as it leaks through the hands.

Imagine this, murmur.
The epochal and the apocryphal.
The dune shifting and the planet lying low tonight
under stars the cars drift westward and the cars
are in heaven and driven by angels.

Imagine this, murmur.
For it is night. Your speech is low.
It is the door and the window. It says
to go out is not to spread a name
but be host to the power of what is in between.

Murmur, imagine this.
Only shining white infinite but not known.
In its heat a sentence murmurs
the secret of transparency is
the opacity of its halo.
Light over all. Light falling through
the graphs of light that are silent and on fire.

Gesture Toward a Glyph of Stars

Sidereal drift. She says:
the names for objects are still pending.

To move through a room is a speech-act.
She says:

The names for things subside
inside of things.

Sub-vocal dissonance.
Continual hum.

She says: parlance of ghosts
their easy murmur, their theater of whispers.

Play of mourning whose center is
everywhere the word has fallen.

A Song of Degrees (I)

This is a song of approach.
Relation. Radiation.
This is a song of ascent.
Nascence. Decryption.

Bring to the eyes of the dead
Al-gebra, that is, restoration.
Petals of a rosary for the finger that wore copper.
Luster of the tablets of a divinatory grammar.

Because the maneuvers of decay sift astral logics
& you must resist taxonomy.
Because a catalogue of cause & effect
is also a secret description of wonder.

Speak therefore as other.
Weird module of sound singeing
the edge of the shelter where
the human is held to, shattered, held to.

(CHARITY AS ENIGMA)

Because he comes at
rates of speed.
Precipitous.
Pronoun as a guide
to wings.
The burnished lathe
of lap of distance.
Because the constant is
a fiction and as such
is undergone.
Because forms accelerated
suffer binarism.
They undergo.
They collapse.
As a frame relay cloud
might make the link.
It could be a sky.
It could be a node.
It could be the entire system
On Fire.
Because the moment carries
a signal into itself.
He dons the beauty
of the waves,
so, so

PLEASURES OF THE LYRIC BODY
for Ingrid Nelson

By the devotion of a smile will you be dethroned.
Skin that is a brightness & contagion.
      The entire force of the body
      hung in the
            fineness of
            what falls
            the eyes contain
            a secret
            that is the
            translation
            of your name
            into water.

Your hair a pageant
            of the impossible.
As the nakedness of the Book
            refutes & affirms all language.

You talk but I'm not listening
            because your hair hangs in a certain way
              & because your eyes.

So the body
            into the very knot of
      song. Plenum & vibration
            migrant with
            the afternoon.

      Because the poem calls for something beyond.
Because skin is
     the vector for every rhyme. As hopeless as
      the word for
      broken.
Because you are gone inside a list
  that is another form of speeding through
  the abandoned
    wreck of summer.

    Behave as if
    a wand
    shook each tree
    to splendor.

TREMBLE
>   (for Anne Waldman and Ed Bowes)

Trembling from the trembling of the other
and trembling with the trembling of desire
for what cannot come as satisfaction
what goes beyond the longing for it
except in calling out the body shivers
there is no other answer except to move
in the love of whatever comes and unseals us.
Valve as the pressure to go under moan
>   or utter wave & sever.

For the annulling of self is necessity
and by it the separate hinges move
in oils of speech & petals. Infinite alteration
beckons from the street or window.
Desire is the truth of desire as neither self nor
what self reaches. To be precisely other
in the vowel of this description means there is
no other utterance for by desire we are never
>   ended & what you gave glows yet.

But as the world is a waking to the other
who arrives and carries in a look what
uncovers me to my self, so I am witness
to the long loosening of the tremble, to its
rain-drenched, gold-planished crossing
of a wing with a branch. Inside such giving
is a becoming again out of lack. And desire
is the strophe. To send & replenish the other
>   who trembles, in a river, always comes back.

A Song of Degrees (ii)

Lyric, the river
    & a speech of sheer silver
    as if time stoned the phrase
    of its misery
    with a bird's tongue
    slivered by fire

Eyes dazed
    by the gift of living/amended
    with a braid of hair
    his hair the summons
    for weather that makes my perfect
    sailing pendant

O love the City
    and the god she builds
    my speech, my canopy, my capital
    music laid through falling
    tones amends
    the faith through intricate folds

Robes, or scrolls
    unrolling over
    what the sky makes
    from fire & builds
    the perfect soul of wood
    drugged, as a river

Who loves me, who seeds me
    who still with seven
    songs retrieves me
    unrescinded
    sinned carefully
    these songs, ascended

In a Somer Seson

Of fire to fire renew
summer the fall
of light and season
of mortal dews.

Overall the evening
set of moon
August high in the trees
equatorial burn.

Grass under green water
& cycle of song
in circle renew
fire of summer to summon

Or signal the fade
of the long moon that burns.
Orbit of fire alive
under green water too.

A Song of Degrees (III)

But to fall in love with the music
as it writes the garden is to be

the one set free among the things
left behind by the dead, all

they had owned
and given to the air

beginning or ending the ladder
of an animal who is song

there is no such thing
as song, you said

unless it is snow falling
from so high only its shadow

reaches us where we stand
inside the weather of its promise

the thought of always
leaving or just arriving

rising up through
the world and its windows

a sound in search of
what does not vanish

but always disappears in the last stanza
the room is for not knowing

but breathing the meaning of
its occasion the cold

evening where we sing
alone

holding to the chant
for disbelieving the stars

Envoi

And then of wind
        strewn in arcs
what wind, I said, could graft
        light to wood?

Strum of thorn
        in bones
& amen moan the rosaries
        of the stylus.

Given length of water
        its westness
all lights founder.
        Shone down on us

splinters & hazards.
        Canopian watch-fire
for the wilderness
        of words.

End Notes

"I have no doubt that in a remoter antiquity the roots of language were regarded as sacred, and when chanted every letter was supposed to stir into motion or evoke some subtle force in the body."
    A.E. (George Russell)

"The one who will shine in the science of writing will shine like the sun."
    anonymous scribe (quoted in Derrida's *Of Grammatology*)

What is a gnostic frequency? And how do we hear one? Is it the poem we tune into, in the dark? The strange language in the middle of the way, on route, that speaks from the other side of knowing, the voice (who speaks?) that murmurs, in the middle of the night, from within not-knowing, out of hope for another kind of knowing? The poem that desires, above everything else, some small vision of *the otherwise*?

This is a book of poems about tuning into the hidden legacies and hermetic inheritances of modernism. A book of endarkening, as Duncan might put it, of a way of knowing that is encrypted, not in musty séances and etiolated rituals, but in the quickening mysteries of logos as it arises from, yields to, and reshapes matter. Becoming gnostic means listening to the heretical speech of the caesura, to the extravagant pulses and rhythms of the unspeakable as it swirls about us, allowing language itself to speak.

The poems of *Gnostic Frequencies* pay tribute to the thread of hermeticism that runs from high modernism to postmodernism. They make special demands of the reader in as much as they ask her to undergo an immersion in the a-signifying stream of language as though it were a form of rhapsodomancy. A gnostic poetics (always lower-case) militates against positivism, against totality, against knowing-as-such. Such a stance invites charges of obscurantism. But what gnostic poetics really calls for is not a reading of the world, but a way to undergo it.

Gnostic Frequencies is built loosely around an earlier document, the 1919 spiritual treatise *Doctrines of the Subtle Body* by British Theosophist G.R.S. Mead. Mead served as secretary to the legendary (some would say, infamous) founder of Theosophy, the Russian émigré Madame Blavatsky during the last years of her life. More importantly, for the history of literary modernism, he befriended and published the poems and essays of Yeats and Pound, who were avid readers of Mead's work on ancient mystery cults. Drawing on a variety of writings from antiquity that range from the Chaldeans to the Gnostics, Mead's book outlines a theory of the so-called subtle body: a kind of transcorporeal, but distinctly material, force field, "the exteriorization of an invisible subtle embodiment of the life of the mind."

Gnostic Frequencies does not address this theory of metaphysics, however. Instead, it takes it up as a metaphor (not unlike, perhaps, the way Yeats funneled the spirit writing of his canny wife George into his poetry). It is a poetic essay that treats semiology as though it were a species of shamanism and shamanism as a branch of semiotics. While poetry reconfigures the affective registers of loss, it also continually constructs and dissolves the ligatures linking Logos to the body.

As a "subtle body," a poem can be thought of as a prostheses of the human sensorium. It extends the range of cognitive possibility through self-evolving forms. Theurgy, the mystical rites advocated by the Neoplatonic thinker Iamblichus, uses song to invoke the theophanic, the showing forth of divine presence, or what today we might be more apt to call a cognitive entanglement with complexity.

The poems here are saturated in, but by no means anchored, to their hermetic and modernist sources. Mead, Yeats, Pound, H.D.; the Enneads, the Chaldean Oracles, the Egyptian mysteries, Iamblichus; Merleau-Ponty and Derrida; all are touchstones and departure points. In this book I have tried to make an image of the Book. Not the house of spirit, but the spirit of house, the poem of the builded place, where the storage, retrieval, and transmission of the letter generates an exteriorized theophanic force field. By theophanic, I don't mean the *a priori* transcendent so much as the messianic rescue of time by language. It is the site where the dead commune with the not-yet, the place of pure potentiality. This is another meaning of the subtle body.

Shadowing many of the poems, especially in Part 1, which is a kind of journal kept by Ariel, is the Library of Alexandria, the largest and most famous of the ancient world. Built by the command of Ptolemy Soter, a former general of Alexander the Great, around 300 B.C., under the directorships of its first two great librarians, Zenodotus, and the poet Callimachus, it was the first library to make its mission the acquisition of volumes on every conceivable subject, from Homer to cookbooks. As the pre-eminent center of learning for several centuries, the library attracted the greatest scholars in the world. Euclid wrote his *Elements* here, while Erastothenes calculated the circumference of the earth to within a few miles of its actual figure. It was here also, among the 490,000 scrolls, that the method of alphabetical categorizing was first employed.

Though a dockside branch of the Library suffered damage from fire during Caesar's desperate fight against the Egyptians in 48 B.C. it was not, as Plutarch claimed, destroyed outright. The main library, housed within the Palace Mouseion, continued to operate until around the death of Plotinus, in 270 C.E., when it was burned as a result of heavy fighting between Christian insurrectionists and the Roman emperor Aurelian. Some sources give the date of its destruction as 391 C.E., when Theophilus, Bishop of Alexandria, ordered a pogrom against all pagan works and temples in the city. Nevertheless, the slur that the invading armies of Mohammed were responsible for its conflagration persists to this day.

Theurgy flourished during the era prior to and just after the Library's destruction. Its foremost exponent, Iamblichus, departed from the teaching of Plotinus by insisting that theosis, or the divinization of the human, could not be achieved through reason alone, but required a kind of transcendental performance: "the perfective operation of the unspeakable acts correctly performed, acts which are beyond all understanding; and on the power of the unutterable symbols which are intelligible only to the gods." The crux of these gnostic frequencies lies here – in the unspeakable, the unutterable – in the darkness that surrounds and informs the matter of the poem as logos itself is what emerges, not from spirit, but out of the earth. Whatever escapes language even as it transfigures it.

In assembling my own gnostic archive of ghost words, those ransacked fugitive traces, I have built an elaborate and somewhat messy constellation, searching for what Pound once called, "the perfect rhythm joined to the perfect word." While not complete, the following list of sources, referents, allusions, and borrowings are strewn through the composition of these poems, which I first began in the spring of 2004, in Boulder, Colorado, and completed in Amherst, Massachusetts in the summer of 2011. Taken together, they comprise a haphazard map of my desire to write a postmodern sophianic poem. But any wisdom to be found here will be of a purely musical, self-cancelling, order.

Ezra Pound, H.D., Robert Duncan, Michael Palmer, Arakawa/Gins, Stephane Mallarme, Andre Breton, Plotinus, Jacques Derrida, G.R.S. Mead, Lawrence Durrell, Odysseas Elytis, Selah Stetie, Doris Lessing, the Corpus Hermeticum, Roger Zelazny, E.M. Forster, Iamblichus, Petrarch, Irigaray, Sir Thomas Browne, Maurice Merleau-Ponty, W.B. Yeats, the Zohar, Jean-Louis Chretien, Rilke, Walter Benjamin, Yves Bonnefoy, Wallace Stevens, Henry Vaughan, Clark Coolidge, Helmholtz, Geoffrey Hill, St.-John Perse, George Oppen, Jean-Luc Nancy, Albert Camus, Simone Weil, Teilhard de Chardin, John Wieners, John Dee, Iain M. Banks, Jacob Boehme, Henri Corbin, Virginia Woolf, and Nathaniel Mackey.

Patrick Pritchett is the author of *Burn, Lives of the Poets, Antiphonal,* and *Salt, My Love.* He serves on the advisory editorial board of Journal of Modern Literature and is a Lecturer in the History and Literature Program at Harvard University and Visiting Lecturer in Poetry at Amherst College.

SPUYTEN DUYVIL
Meeting Eyes Bindery
Triton
Lithic Scatter

8TH AVENUE   Stefan Brecht
A DAY AND A NIGHT AT THE BATHS   Michael Rumaker
ACTS OF LEVITATION   Laynie Browne
ALIEN MATTER   Regina Derieva
ANARCHY   Mark Scroggins
APO/CALYPSO   Gordon Osing
APPLES OF THE EARTH   Dina Elenbogen
ARC: CLEAVAGE OF GHOSTS   Noam Mor
THE ARSENIC LOBSTER   Peter Grandbois
AUNTIE VARVARA'S CLIENTS   Stelian Tanase
BALKAN ROULETTE   Drazan Gunjaca
THE BANKS OF HUNGER AND HARDSHIP   J. Hunter Patterson
BLACK LACE   Barbara Henning
BIRD ON THE WING   Juana Culhane
BREATHING BOLAÑO   Thilleman & Blevins
BREATHING FREE   (ed.) Vyt Bakaitis
BURIAL SHIP   Nikki Stiller
BUTTERFLIES   Brane Mozetic
BY THE TIME YOU FINISH THIS BOOK
        YOU MIGHT BE DEAD   Aaron Zimmerman
CAPTIVITY NARRATIVES   Richard Blevins
CELESTIAL MONSTER   Juana Culhane
CLEOPATRA HAUNTS THE HUDSON   Sarah White
COLUMNS: TRACK 2   Norman Finkelstein
CONSCIOUSNESS SUITE   David Landrey
THE CONVICTION & SUBSEQUENT
        LIFE OF SAVIOR NECK   Christian TeBordo
CONVICTION'S NET OF BRANCHES   Michael Heller
THE CORYBANTES   Tod Thilleman
CROSSING BORDERS   Kowit & Silverberg

DAY BOOK OF A VIRTUAL POET   Robert Creeley
DAYLIGHT TO DIRTY WORK   Tod Thilleman
THE DESIRE NOTEBOOKS   John High
DETECTIVE SENTENCES   Barbara Henning
DIARY OF A CLONE   Saviana Stanescu
DIFFIDENCE   Jean Harris
DONNA CAMERON   Donna Cameron
DON'T KILL ANYONE, I LOVE YOU   Gojmir Polajnar
DRAY-KHMARA AS A POET   Oxana Asher
EGGHEAD TO UNDERHOOF   Tod Thilleman
EROTICIZING THE NATION   Leverett T. Smith, Jr.
THE EVIL QUEEN   Benjamin Perez
EXTREME POSITIONS   Stephen Bett
THE FARCE   Carmen Firan
FISSION AMONG THE FANATICS   Tom Bradley
THE FLAME CHARTS   Paul Oppenheimer
FLYING IN WATER   Barbara Tomash
FORM   Martin Nakell
GESTURE THROUGH TIME   Elizabeth Block
GHOSTS!   Martine Bellen
GIRAFFES IN HIDING   Carol Novack
GOD'S WHISPER   Dennis Barone
GOWANUS CANAL, HANS KNUDSEN   Tod Thilleman
HALF-GIRL   Stephanie Dickinson
HIDDEN DEATH, HIDDEN ESCAPE   Liviu Georgescu
HOUNDSTOOTH   David Wirthlin
IDENTITY   Basil King
IN TIMES OF DANGER   Paul Oppenheimer
INCRETION   Brian Strang
INFERNO   Carmen Firan
INFINITY SUBSECTIONS   Mark DuCharme
INSOUCIANCE   Thomas Phillips
INVERTED CURVATURES   Francis Raven
JACKPOT   Tsipi Keller
THE JAZZER & THE LOITERING LADY   Gordon Osing

KNOWLEDGE   Michael Heller
LADY V.   D.R. Popa
LAST SUPPER OF THE SENSES   Dean Kostos
A LESSER DAY   Andrea Scrima
LET'S TALK ABOUT DEATH   M. Maurice Abitbol
LIGHT HOUSE   Brian Lucas
LIGHT YEARS: MULTIMEDIA IN THE EAST
        VILLAGE, 1960-1966   (ed.) Carol Bergé
LITTLE BOOK OF DAYS   Nona Caspers
LITTLE TALES OF FAMILY & WAR   Martha King
LONG FALL: ESSAYS AND TEXTS   Andrey Gritsman
LUNACIES   Ruxandra Cesereanu
LUST SERIES   Stephanie Dickinson
LYRICAL INTERFERENCE   Norman Finkelstein
MAINE BOOK   Joe Cardarelli (ed.) Anselm Hollo
MANNHATTeN   Sarah Rosenthal
MATING IN CAPTIVITY   Nava Renek
MEANWHILE   Gordon Osing
MEDIEVAL OHIO   Richard Blevins
MEMORY'S WAKE   Derek Owens
MERMAID'S PURSE   Laynie Browne
MOBILITY LOUNGE   David Lincoln
THE MOSCOVIAD   Yuri Andrukhovych
MULTIFESTO: A HENRI D'MESCAN READER   Davis Schneiderman
NO PERFECT WORDS   Nava Renek
NO WRONG NOTES   Norman Weinstein
NORTH & SOUTH   Martha King
NOTES OF A NUDE MODEL   Harriet Sohmers Zwerling
OF ALL THE CORNERS TO FORGET   Gian Lombardo
OUR FATHER   M.G. Stephens
OVER THE LIFELINE   Adrian Sangeorzan
PART OF THE DESIGN   Laura E. Wright
PIECES FOR SMALL ORCHESTRA & OTHER FICTIONS   Norman Lock
A PLACE IN THE SUN   Lewis Warsh
THE POET : PENCIL PORTRAITS   Basil King

Political Ecosystems   J.P. Harpignies
Powers: Track 3   Norman Finkelstein
Prurient Anarchic Omnibus   j/j Hastain
Retelling   Tsipi Keller
Rivering   Dean Kostos
Root-Cellar to Riverine   Tod Thilleman
The Roots of Human Sexuality   M. Maurice Abitbol
Saigon and other poems   Jack Walters
A Sardine on Vacation   Robert Castle
Savoir Fear   Charles Borkhuis
Secret of White   Barbara Tomash
Seduction   Lynda Schor
See What You Think   David Rosenberg
Settlement   Martin Nakell
Sex and the Senior City   M. Maurice Abitbol
Slaughtering the Buddha   Gordon Osing
The Snail's Song   Alta Ifland
The Spark Singer   Jade Sylvan
Spiritland   Nava Renek
Strange Evolutionary Flowers   Lizbeth Rymland
Suddenly Today We Can Dream   Rutha Rosen
The Sudden Death of...   Serge Gavronsky
The Takeaway Bin   Toni Mirosevich
Talking God's Radio Show   John High
Tautological Eye   Martin Nakell
Ted's Favorite Skirt   Lewis Warsh
Things That Never Happened   Gordon Osing
Thread   Vasyl Makhno
Three Mouths   Tod Thilleman
Three Sea Monsters   Tod Thilleman
Track   Norman Finkelstein
Transitory   Jane Augustine
Transparencies Lifted From Noon   Chris Glomski

Tsim-tsum   Marc Estrin
Vienna ØØ   Eugene K. Garber
Uncensored Songs for Sam Abrams   (ed.) John Roche
Warp Spasm   Basil King
Watchfulness   Karen Lillis
Watch The Doors As They Close   Karen Lillis
Walking After Midnight   Bill Kushner
West of West End   Peter Freund
When the Gods Come Home to Roost   Marc Estrin
Whirligig   Christopher Salerno
White, Christian   Christopher Stoddard
Winter Letters   Vasyl Makhno
Within the Space Between   Stacy Cartledge
A World of Nothing But Nations   Tod Thilleman
A World of Nothing But Self-Infliction   Tod Thilleman
Wreckage of Reason   (ed.) Nava Renek
the Yellow House   Robin Behn
You, Me, and the Insects   Barbara Henning

www.ingramcontent.com/pod-product-compliance
Lightning Source LLC
Chambersburg PA
CBHW032122090426
42743CB00007B/431